Reminiscences
of
Wordsworth
among
the
Peasantry
of
Westmoreland

Reminiscences of Wordsworth among the Peasantry of Westmoreland

Hardwicke Drummond Rawnsley

With an introduction by Geoffrey Tillotson

Dillon's London

Text © 1968 Jackson Son & Co. Ltd.
Professor Tillotson's introduction:
© 1968 Dillon's University Bookshop Ltd

Library of Congress number: 68–57934
Standard Book Number: 900333 00 6

Introduction

IN MAY 1882 the Rev. Hardwicke Drummond Rawnsley, who later became known as Canon Rawnsley and who with Octavia Hill and Robert Hunter founded the National Trust, contributed a paper to the *Transactions of the Wordsworth Society*. When he collected it in his *Lake Country Sketches* of 1903 he had revised it in small ways. His revisions bring the speech of the Lakelanders nearer to their dialect and so take it further away from the standard speech. Reminiscences can never be quite accurate. They are always accepted by their readers as having been trimmed and coloured for the sake of looking as presentable as possible. The text of 1903 therefore completes the process carried some way in the text of 1882. It is this revised text that is here reprinted.

These reminiscences of Wordsworth are inevitably of the 'later' Wordsworth, who had died in 1850 at the age of 80. They show him to be living in a region, but not fully. He is not fully in or of the human part of it. This might surprise readers of the earlier Wordsworth because several famous or notorious poems written around the turn of the century— conspicuously 'Goody Blake and Harry Gill', 'Simon Lee, the Old Huntsman', and the 'Idiot Boy' among the Lyrical Ballads and the great *Prelude* itself—show that as a boy and younger man he had belonged to that region fully and closely. From the evidence collected by Rawnsley, we gather that the only thing shared between the later Wordsworth and the shepherds, blacksmiths and so on of the locality was an interest in the erection of buildings, in trees as trees are somebody's property, and in skating. (We learn that he had once been present at a wrestling match but apparently by accident, and that, though he enjoyed the spectacle, he did not trouble to attend another). The explanation of this withdrawal as an older man is that by the time he was fully middle-aged— say by 1815, the date of the *Excursion*—he had learned all he needed to know from individuals, even including himself. Peasants especially had now no more to teach him. In the *Prelude* he had said that 'shepherds were the men that pleased me first', but what had come to please him in later years were men in the aggregate. He said that he 'had given twelve hours' thought to the conditions and prospects of society for one to poetry'. His maturer instincts lay in what we should now call sociology, politics, economics, psychology, and so on, and in these things as they have become subjects of study in our twentieth-century Universities. His interests had become those that were soon to flame out in Carlyle. Wordsworth, like him, was concerned with the 'condition-of-England' question, and the main use he now had as a poet and letter-writer for individuals was as they contributed light to these interests. He had shed some of his concern with men as creatures of a 'pleasing anxious being', as creatures who feel what comes to them as men, distinct from what comes to them as workers, as members of a social and economic community. In the early poems these strong later interests were already in existence, and abundantly. All his 'peasant' poetry had shown him a thinker, alert to economic facts. 'Goody Blake and Harry Gill' is a great human poem partly because Wordsworth had keenly felt the conditions under which the old woman lived. That poem tells how one winter Goody Blake was so cold that she stole twigs out of the hedge of Gill, the wealthy cattle dealer, in order to have a fire. When he contrived to catch her red-handed, she cursed him as he deserved to be cursed, and with a curse that proved effective:

> She pray'd, her withered hand, uprearing,
> While Harry held her by the arm—
> 'God! Who art never out of hearing,
> O may he nevermore be warm!'
> The cold, cold moon above her head,
> Thus on her knees did Goody pray.
> Young Harry heard what she had said,
> And icy cold he turned away.

And that leads to the end of Harry. There is much feeling in

the poem—or rather in between its lines—because Words-
worth had identified himself with Goody Blake as a human
being complete. He tells us all the important things that a
present-day social worker would have elicited by his question-
naire! She was 'ill-fed' and 'thinly clad', a spinner 'all day . . . in
her poor dwelling', and with little to show for it:

> Alas, 'twas hardly worth the telling—[counting]
> It would not pay for candlelight,
> —This woman dwelt in Dorsetshire,
> Her hut was on a cold hill side
> And in that country coals are dear,
> For they come far by wind and tide,

—presumably by water from Co. Durham. And there is more
of the painful knowledge in what follows:

> By the same fire to boil their pottage
> Two poor old dames, as I have known,
> Will often live in one small cottage;
> But she poor woman! dwelt alone.
> 'Twas well enough when summer came
> The long, warm, lightsome summer day,
> Then at her door the *canty* dame
> Would sit, as any linnet gay.

'As I have known', he says, and in that line about the summer
day he specifies the three things that mattered most in the
twenty-four hours for a cottage spinner. Goody herself, even
if blessed with the intelligence of the Lakelanders of these
reminiscences, could not have given a more telling account of
her way of life. And the young Wordsworth joined her in her
feelings about it all. He soon exhausted, however, what he
could learn about the peasants and lower orders generally
because, as Gray noted, their 'annals' are 'short and simple'.
If he was aloof in later life that was because what he had once
humbly learned from them had long ago become merged in a
vastly bigger matter—in the present condition of England.
Unlike the young Wordsworth, the older man felt no call on
his feelings, except towards man in the aggregate.

Then again, his life-long interest in the rocks and stones and trees of the neighbourhood had far outsoared the peasants' interests in them. For Wordsworth such things had become the 'instruments of his religion'—to borrow a phrase of Sterne's. In his later years he had fully become, as Arnold testified, 'a priest to us all Of the wonder and bloom of the world'. That phrase 'us all' was an exaggeration. It meant no more than 'us who read my poem'. It did not include the common folk. Wordsworth's poetry had performed no holy office for them.

And if he had little further use for them, they in their turn had use for him only as a curiosity for their open-eyed observance. Johnson had said that Swift had 'expired a driveller and a show'. And something not very different might have been said of Wordsworth, aloof in his egotistical sublimity. For the peasants, as they themselves depose, poetry, unless of the ribald sort they found in their chapbooks, and its practitioners were as remote as the moon, and far less useful.

And yet, all of them were poets themselves. Only poetical writers can use words as they could. What satirists they would have made—or rather what satirists they were, without knowing it! The speech of Rawnsley is a pale thing beside theirs.

GEOFFREY TILLOTSON

Reminiscences of Wordsworth

HAVING GROWN UP in the neighbourhood of Alfred Tennyson's old home in Lincolnshire, I had been struck with the swiftness with which,

> As year by year the labourer tills
> His wonted glebe, or lops the glades,

the memories of the poet of the Somersby Wold had faded 'from off the circle of the hills.' I had been astonished to note how little real interest was taken in him or his fame, and how seldom his works were met with in the houses of the rich or poor in the very neighbourhood.

It was natural that, coming to reside in the Lake country, I should endeavour to find out what of Wordsworth's memory among the men of the Dales still lingered on,—how far he was still a moving presence among them,—how far his works had made their way into the cottages and farm-houses of the valleys.

But if a certain love of the humorous induced me to enter into or follow up conversations with the few still living among the peasants who were in the habit of seeing Wordsworth in the flesh, there was also a genuine wish to endeavour to find out how far the race of Westmoreland and Cumberland farm-folk—the 'Matthews' and the 'Michaels' of the poet as described by him—were real or fancy pictures, or how far the characters of the dalesmen had been altered in any remarkable manner by tourist influences during the thirty-two years that have passed since the aged poet was laid to rest.

For notwithstanding the fact that Mr. Ruskin, writing in 1876, had said 'that the Border peasantry (painted with absolute fidelity by Scott and Wordsworth)' are, as hitherto, a scarcely injured race,—that in his fields at Coniston he had men who might have fought with Henry V at Agincourt without being distinguished from any of his knights,—that he could take his tradesmen's word for a thousand pounds, and need never latch his garden gate, nor fear molestation in wood or on moor, for his girl guests; the more one went about seeking for such good life and manners and simple piety as Wordsworth knew and described in fell-side homes, or such generous unselfishness and nobility among the Dale farmers as would seem to have been contemporaries of the poet, the more one was a little saddened to find a characteristic something faded away, and a certain beauty vanished that the simple retirement of old valley-days of fifty years ago gave to the men amongst whom Wordsworth lived. The strangers with their gifts of gold, their vulgarity, and their requirements, have much to answer for in the matter. But it is true that the decent exterior, the shrewd wit, and the manly independence and natural knightliness of the men of the soil is to a large extent responsible for raising expectations of nobility of life and morals, the expectation of which would be justified by no other peasant class in England, and which, by raising an unfair standard for comparison, ought to be prepared for some disappointment. All said and done they are Nature's gentlefolk still.

One's walks and talks with the few who remember Words-worth, or *Wudsworth* as they always call him, have done little to find out more than the impression that they as outsiders formed of him, but it allowed one to grasp by the hand a few of those natural noblemen who by their presence still give testimony to a time and a race of men and women fast fading away, and in need already of the immortality of lofty tradition that Wordsworth has accorded them.

While these few of his still living peasant contemporaries show us the sort of atmosphere of severely simple life, hand-in-hand with a 'joy in wildest commonalty spread,' that made some of Wordsworth's poems possible, I think the facts that they seem to establish of Wordsworth's seclusion, and the distance he seems to have kept from them and their cottage homes, not a little interesting. For they point to the suggestion that the poet lived so separate and apart from them, so seldom entered the 'huts where poor men lie,' or mixed with the fell-side folk at their sports and junketings, that he was enabled, in his swift selection and appreciation of the good and pure and true in their surroundings, to forget, quite honestly perhaps, the faults of the people among whom he lived.

Be that as it may, this paper aims at establishing no new doctrine or view about the man, but at simply putting on record reminiscences still in the minds of some of those who often saw him, knew his fancies and his ways (as only servants know the fancies and ways of their master), and spoke with him sixty, fifty, or forty years ago.[1]

These reminiscences may seem worthless to many, just from the fact that they are the words of outsiders. They will seem to others of interest for that very reason. And this much must be said, they are trustworthy records from true mouths. The native love of *truth*, or perhaps better, the native *dislike ever to hazard suggestion*, or to speak *without book*, is guarantee for that. To ask questions in Westmoreland is the reverse of asking them of Syrian fellaheen and Egyptian dragomans. The Cumberland mind is not inventive, nor swift to anticipate the answer you wish, and one is always brought up sharp with—

'Nay, I wadnt say that nayther':
'Nay, I'se not sartain aboot that':
'Might bea, but not to my knowledge howivver:
'Its nea good my saaing I kna that, when I doant, noo than,'
—and so on.

Twenty summers had let the daisies blossom round Wordsworth's grave, when, in 1870, I heard of and saw the old lady who had once been in service at Rydal Mount, and was now a lodging-house keeper at Grasmere. She shall be called as first witness, but what kind of practical and unimaginative mind she had may be gathered from the following anecdote. My sister came in from a late evening walk, and said, 'O Mrs. D——, have you seen the wonderful sun set?' The good lady turned sharply round, and drawing herself to her full height, as if mortally offended, answered, 'No, Miss R——, I'm a tidy cook, I know, and, 'they say,' a decentish body for

[1]This paper was written in 1881 and was read at the annual meeting of the Wordsworth Society in London in 1882—Robert Browning in the chair.

a landlady, and sic-like, but I nivver bodder nowt aboot sunsets or them sort of things, they're nowt ataw i' my line.' Her reminiscence of Wordsworth was as worthy of tradition as it was explanatory, from her point of view, of the method in which Wordsworth composed, and was helped in his labours by his enthusiastic sister.

'Well you kna,' were her words, 'Mr. Wordsworth went bumming and booing about, and she, Miss Dorothy, kept close behint him, and she picked up the bits as he let 'em fall, and tak 'em down, and put 'em on paper for him. And you med,' continued the good dame, 'be very well sure as how she didn't understand nor make sense out of 'em, and I doubt that he [Wordsworth] didn't kna much aboot them either himself, but, howivver, there's a gay lock o' fowk as wad, I dar say.'

And here it will be well to put in a caution. The vernacular of the Lake district must be understood a little, or wrong impressions would be got of the people's memory of the bard. 'What was Mr. Wordsworth like in personal appearance?' I once asked of an old retainer, who still lives not far from Rydal Mount. 'He was a ugly-faäced man, and a meän liver,' was the answer. And when he continued, 'Ay, and he was a deäl aboot t' roads, ye kna,' one might have been pardoned if one had concluded that the Lake poet was a sort of wild man of the woods, an ugly customer of desperate life, or highwayman of vagrant habit. All that was really meant when translated was, that he was a man of marked features, and led a very simple life in matters of food and raiment.

The next witness I shall call to speak of the poet is none other than the lad whose wont it was to serve the Rydal Mount kitchen with meat, week in week out, in the poet's days. A grey-haired man himself now, his chief memory of Wordsworth is that of a tall man, 'rather a fineish man in build, with a bit of a stoop, and a deal of grey hair upon his heäd.' In some of the days of close analysis that are coming upon us, poets will perhaps be found to have depended for the particular colour of their poems, or turns and cast of thought, upon the kind of food—vegetable or animal—that they mostly subsisted on. It will be well to chronicle the fact that Wordsworth had an antipathy to veal, but was very partial to legs—'lived on legs, you med amost say.' But as my friend added, almost in the same breath, that the poet was a 'greät walker i' t' daäles,' he had uttered unconsciously a double truth.

The next fact that remained clear and distinct in the butcher's mind was, that whenever you met the poet he was sure to be 'quite [pronounced white] pläinly dressed.' Sometimes in a round blue cloak; sometimes wearing a big wideawake, or a bit of an old boxer, but plainly dressed, almost 'poorly dressed, ya mun saay, at the best o' times.' 'But for aw that, he was quite an object man,' he added, meaning that there was a dignity that needed no dressing to set it off, I suppose, in the poet's mien and manner. It was interesting to hear, too, how different Wordsworth had seemed in his grave silent way of passing children without a word, from 'li'le Hartley Coleridge,' with his constant salutation, uncertain gait, his head on one side, his walking-stick suddenly shouldered, and then his frantic little rushes along the road, between the pauses of his thought. 'Many's the time,' said my friend, 'that me and my sister has run ourselves intil a lather to git clear fra Hartley, for we allays thowt, ya kna, when he started running he was efter us. But as fur Mister Wudsworth, he'd pass you, same as if yan was nobbut a stean. He niver cared for childer, however; yan may be certain of that, for didn't I have to pass him four times in t' week, up to the door wi' meat? And he niver oncst said owt. Ye're well aware, if he'd been fond of children he 'ud 'a spoke.'

But Mrs. Wordsworth had made her impressions too on the youth's mind. 'As for Mrs. Wudsworth, she was pläiner in her ways than he was. The pläinest wooman in these parts, —for aw the warld the bettermer part of an auld farm-body.' He intended nothing disrespectful by this simile, he only wished to say she was simple in manner and dress. But if

Mrs. Wordsworth's personal appearance had impressed him, her powers of housekeeping had impressed him more. She was very persevering, and 'terb'le particular in her accounts, never allowed you an inch in the butching-book.' It did not raise one's opinion of Lake country butcher morality to find this a grievance, but the man as he spoke seemed to think a little sorely of those old-fashioned days, when mistresses, not cooks, took supervision of the household economies.

I bade my friend good-day, and the last words I heard were, 'But Mr. Wudsworth *was quite an object man, mind ye.*'

It is an easy transition from butcher-boy to gardener's lad, and I will now detail a conversation I had with one who, in this latter capacity at Rydal Mount, saw the poet daily for some years.

It was Easter Monday, and I knew that the one-time gardener's lad at Rydal Mount had grown into a vale-renowned keeper of a vale-renowned beer-house. I had doubts as to calling on this particular day, for Easter Monday and beer go much together in our Lake country. But I was half reassured by a friend who said, 'Well, he gets drunk three times a day, but taks t' air atween whiles, and if you catch him airing he will be verra civil, but it's a bad day to find him sober, this.' I explained that I wanted to talk with him of old Wordsworthian days. 'Aw, it's Wudsworth you're a gaan to see about? If that's the game, you're reet enuff, for, drunk or sober, he can crack away a deal upon Mr. Wudsworth. An' i'se not so varry seuer but what he's best drunk a li'le bit.' I was reassured, and soon found myself sitting on the stone ale-bench outside the public-house, the best of friends with a man who had been apparently grossly libelled—for he was as sober as a judge—and whose eye fairly twinkled as he spoke of the Rydal garden days.

'You see, blessed barn, it's a lock o' daäys sin', but I remember them daäys, for I was put by my master to the Rydal Mount as gardener-boy to keep me fra bad waays. And I remember one John Wudsworth, Mr. Wudsworth's nevi, parson he was, dëad, like eneuf, afore this. Well, he was stayin' there along o' his missus, first week as I was boy there, and I was ter'ble curious, and was like enough to hev bin drowned, for they had a bath, filled regular o' nights, up above, ya kna, with a sort of curtainment all round it. And blowed if I didn't watch butler fill it, and then goa in and pull string, and down came t' watter, and I was 'maazed as owt, and I screamed, and Mr. John come and fun' me, and saäved my life. Eh, blessed barn, them was daäys lang sen'.'

I asked whether Mr. Wordsworth was much thought of. He replied, 'Latterly, but we thowt li'le eneuf on him. He was nowt to li'le Hartley. Li'le Hartley was a philosopher, you see; Wudsworth was a poet. Ter'ble girt difference betwixt them two wayses, ye kna.' I asked whether he had ever found that poems of Mr. Wordsworth were read in the cottages, whether he had read them himself. 'Well you see, blessed barn, there's pomes and pomes, and Wudsworth's was not for sec as us. I never did see his pomes—not as I can speak to in any man's house in these parts, but,' he added, 'ye kna there's bits in t' papers fra time to time bearing his naame.'

This unpopularity of Wordsworth's poems among the peasantry was strangely corroborated that very same day by an old man whom I met on the road, who said he had often seen the poet, and had once been present and heard him make a long speech, and that was at the laying of the foundation of the Boys' Schoolroom at Bowness, which was built by one Mr. Bolton of Storrs Hall.

On that occasion Mr. 'Wudsworth talked lang and weel eneuf,' and he remembered that he 'had put a pome he had written into a bottle wi' some coins in the hollow of the foundation-stone.'

I asked him whether he had ever seen or read any of the poet's works, and he answered, 'Nay, not likely; for Wudsworth wasn't a man as wreat on separate bits, saäme as Hartley Coleridge, and was niver a frequenter of public-houses, or owt of that sort.' But he added, 'He was a good writer, he supposed, and he was a man folks thowt a deal on i' t' dale: he was sic a weel-meäning, decent, quiet man.'

But to return to my host at the public. Wordsworth, in his opinion, was not fond of children, nor animals. He would come round the garden, but never 'say nowt.' Sometimes, but this was seldom, he would say, 'Oh! you're planting peas?' or, 'Where are you setting onions?' but only as a master would ask a question of a servant. He had, he said, never seen him out of temper once, neither in the garden, nor when he was along o' Miss Dorothy in her invalid chair. But, he added, 'What went on i' t' hoose I can't speak till'; meaning that as an outdoor servant he had no sufficiently accurate knowledge of the in-door life to warrant his speaking of it. Wordsworth was not an early riser, had no particular flower he was fondest of that he could speak to; never was heard to sing or whistle a tune in his life; there 'was noa two words about that, though he bummed a deäl';—of this more presently.

'He was a plain man, plainly dressed, and so was she, ya mun kna. But eh, blessed barn! he was fond o' his own childer, and fond o' Dorothy, especially when she was faculty strucken, poor thing; and as for his wife, there was noa two words about their being truly companionable; and Wudsworth was a silent man wi'out a doubt, but he was not aboon bein' tender and quite *monstrable* [demonstrative] at times in his oan family.'

I asked about Mr. Wordsworth's powers of observation. Had he noticed in his garden walks how he stooped down and took this or that flower, or smelt this or that herb? (I have heard since that the poet's sense of smell was limited.) 'Na, he wadna speak to that, but Mr. Wudsworth was what you might call a vara practical-eyed man, a man as seemed to see aw that was stirrin'.'

Perhaps the most interesting bit of information I obtained, before our pleasant chat was at an end, was a description of the way in which the poet composed on the grass terrace at Rydal Mount. 'Eh! blessed barn,' my informant continued, 'I think I can see him at it now. He was ter'ble thrang with visitors and folks, you mun kna, at times, but if he could git awa fra them

17

for a spell, he was out upon his gres walk; and then he would set his heäd a bit forrad, and put his hands behint his back. And then he would start a bumming, and it was bum, bum, bum, stop; then bum, bum, bum reet down till t'other end, and then he'd set down and git a bit o' paper out and write a bit; and then he git up, and bum, bum, bum, and goa on bumming for long enough right down and back agean. I suppose, ya kna, the bumming helped him out a bit. However, his lips was always goan' whoale time he was upon the gres walk. He was a kind mon, there's no two words about that: if any one was sick i' the plaace, he wad be off to see til 'em.'

And so ended my Easter Monday talk with the poet's quondam gardener's boy, the now typical beerhouse-keeper, half pleased, half proud, to remember his old master in such service as he rendered him, in the days when it was judged that to keep a boy out of mischief and from bad company it was advisable to get him a place at Rydal Mount.

I must ask you next to take a seat with me in a waller's cottage. If tea and bread and butter is offered, you had better take it also, it is almost sure to be pressed upon you, and it is of the best. I will be interrogator, only by way of introduction saying, that our host is a splendid type of the real Westmoreland gentleman labourer, who was in his days a wrestler too, and whose occupation at the building of *Foxhow* and *Fiddler's Farm* in the Rydal Valley, often allowed him to see the poet in old times.

'Well, George, what sort o' a man in personal appearance was Mr. Wordsworth?'

'He was what you might ca' a ugly man,—mak of John Rigg much,—much about seame height, 6 feet or 6 feet 2,—smaller, but deal rougher in the face.'

I knew John Rigg by sight, and can fancy from the pictures of the poet that the likeness is striking in the brow and profile.

'But he was,' continued George, 'numbledy in t' kneas, walked numbledy, ye kna, but that might o' wussened wi' age.'

In George's mind age accounted for most of the peculiarities

18

he had noticed in the poet, but George's memory could go back fifty years, and he ought to have remembered Wordsworth as hale and hearty. 'He wozn't a man as said a deal to common fwoak. But he talked a deal to hissen. I often seead his lipa a gaäin', and he'd a deal o' mumblin' to hissel, and 'ud stop short and be a lookin' down upo' the ground, as if he was in a thinking waäy. But that might ha' growed on him wi' age, an' aw, ye kna.'

How true, thought I, must have been the poet's knowledge of himself.

> And who is he with modest looks,
> And clad in sober russet gown?
> He murmurs by the running brooks,
> A music sweeter than their own;
> He is retired as noontide dew,
> Or fountain in a noonday grove.

And indeed, in all the reminiscences I have obtained among the peasantry, these lines force themselves upon one as corroborated by their evidence.

'He' [Mr Wordsworth], continued George, 'was a deal upo' the road, would goa moast days to L'Ambleside i' his cloak and umbrella, and in later times fwoaks would stare and gaum to see him pass, not that we thowt much to him hereaboots, but they was straängers, ye see.'

It is curious, though natural perhaps, to find a sort of disbelief among the natives in the poet's greatness, owing somewhat to the fact that it 'was straängers as set such store by him.' They distrust strangers still, almost as much as they did in old Border-times.

But the secret of Wordsworth's unpopularity with the dalesmen seems to have been that he was shy and retired, and not one who mixed freely or talked much with them.

'We woz,' said George, 'noan of us very fond on 'im; eh, dear! quite a different man from li'le Hartley. He wozn't a man as was very compannable, ye kna. He was fond o' steanes and mortar, though,' he added. 'It was in '48, year of revolution, one Frost, they ca'd him rebellious (Monmouth), and a doment in Ireland. I mind we was at wuk at Fiddler's Farm, and Muster Wudsworth 'ud come down maist days, and he sed "it sud be ca'èd Model Farm," and sa it was.'

Speaking of Foxhow, he said, 'He and the Doctor [Dr. Arnold], you've mappen hard tell o' t' Doctor,—well, he and the Doctor was much i' yan anudder's company; and Wudsworth was a girt un for chimleys, had summut to saay in the makkin' of a deal of 'em hereaboot. There was 'maist all the chimleys Rydal way built efter his mind. I can mind he and the Doctor had girt argiments aboot the chimleys time we was building Foxhow, and Wudsworth sed he liked a bit o' colour in 'em. And that the chimley coigns sud be natural headed and natural bedded, a lile bit red and a lile bit yallar. For there is a bit of colour i' t' quarry stean up Easedale way. And heèd a girt fancy an' aw for chimleys square up hauf way, and round t'other. And so we built 'em that road.' It was amusing to find that the house chimney-stacks up Rydal way are in truth so many breathing monuments of the bard. The man who with his face to the Continent passed in that sunny pure July morn of 1803 over Westminster Bridge, and noticed with joy the smokeless air, rejoiced also to sit 'without emotion, hope, or aim, by his half-kitchen and half-parlour fire' at Town End, and wherever he went seems to have noted with an eye of love

> The smoke forth issuing whence and how it may,
> Like wreaths of vapour without stain or blot.

But if from the highland huts he had observed how intermittently the blue smoke-curls rose and fell, he was most pleased to watch on a still day the tremulous upward pillars of smoke that rose from the cottages of his native dale. In his *Guide to the Lakes* (page 44) Wordsworth has said, 'The singular beauty of the chimneys will not escape the eye of the attentive traveller. The low square quadrangular form is often surmounted by a tall cylinder, giving to the cottage chimney the most beautiful shape that is ever seen. Nor will it be too fanciful or refined to remark that there is a pleasing harmony between a tall chimney of this circular form and the living column of smoke ascending from it through the still air.' And my friend George's memory of Mr. Wordsworth's dictum about the need of having the chimney coign 'natural headed and natural bedded, a lile bit red and a lile bit yallar' is again found to be true to the life from a passage in the same *Guide to the Lakes* (p. 60), in which the poet, after stating that the principle that ought to determine the position, size, and architecture of a house (viz., that it should be so constructed as to admit of being incorporated into the scenery of nature) should also determine its colour, goes on to say 'that since the chief defect of colour in the Lake country is an over-prevalence of bluish-tint, to counteract this the colour of houses should be of a warmer tone than the native rock allows'; and adds, 'But where the cold blue tint of the rocks is enriched by an iron tinge, the colours cannot be too closely imitated, and will be produced of itself by the stones hewn from the adjoining quarry.' How beautiful the colouring of the Rydal quarry stone is, and how dutifully the son of the poet carried out his father's will in his recent rebuilding of a family residence near Foxhow, may be judged by all who glance at the cylindrical chimneys, or look at the natural material that forms the panels of the porch of the 'Stepping-stones' under Loughrigg.

I rose to go, but George detained me. For he was proud to remember that upon one occasion Mr. Wudsworth had keenly watched him as he put forth his feats of strength in the wrestling ring at Ambleside, 'in the churchyard, day efter t' fair, forty or fifty years sen,' and had passed a remark upon him. It was in the days 'when fowks wrestled for nowt no mair than a bit o' leather strap.' And George had 'coomed to pit,' as the saying is, and 'Efter comin agaen ya man and throwin' him, and anudder and throwin' him,' was last man in against a noted wrestler, one Tom Chapman. He had agreed for one fall. Mr. Wordsworth was 'leukin' on.' George and his antagonist 'com' together, and Chapman fell. 'And I mind

that I was mair pleased wi' Mr. Wudsworth's word than wi'
t' strap (or belt), for fowks tell't me that he keepit saying,
"He must be a powerful young man that. He must be a strong
young man." '

So ends our chat with honest George, the waller. We will
next interview a man who at one time, for more than eleven
years, saw Wordsworth almost daily. This was in the days
that Hartley Coleridge lived at the Nab Cottage, or, as our
friend puts it (with a touch of menagerie suggestion in it),
'i' t' daays when *he kep' li'le Hartley* at t' Nab,'—for our
friend was Coleridge's landlord. I had considerable difficulty
here, as in almost all my interviews with the good folk, of
keeping to the object or subject in hand. For li'le Hartley's
ghost was always coming to the front. 'Naäy, naäy, I cannot
say a deal to that, but ye kna li'le Hartley would do so-and-so.
Li'le Hartley was t' yan for them. If it had been Hartley, noo,
I could ha' tell't ye a deäl.' And so on.

But in this particular instance my difficulty was trebled, for
my friend evidently nursed the idea that Wordsworth had got
most of 'his potry out of Hartley,' and had in return dealt
very hardly with him, in the matter of admonishment and
advice, while at the same time Mrs. Wordsworth, in her capacity
of common-sense accountant, with a strict dislike to wasteful
expenditure or indiscriminate charity, had left something of
bitter in his cup of Rydal Mount memories; and the old man
would gladly enough pass over a Wordsworth leaflet for a
folio page of li'le Hartley. But he too would be true in his
speech, and would speak as he 'kna'ed,' neither more nor less.
In his judgment Mr. Wordsworth was a 'plainish-faaced man,
but a fine man, tall and lish (active), and allus aboot t' roads.
He wasn't a man o' many words, wad walk by you times
eneuf wi'out sayin' owt particler when he was studyin'. He
was allus studyin' and you med see his lips gaen as he went
aboot t' roads. He did most of his study upo' the roads. I
suppose,' he added, 'he was a cliverish man, but he wasn't
set much on by nin on us. He lent Hartley a deäl o' his beuks,

it's sartain, but Hartley helped him a deäl, I understand, did t' best part o' his poems for him, sae t' sayin' is.'

'He wad often come i' t' efterneun and hev a talk at t' Nab, and would gang oot wi' Hartley takkin' him by t' arm for long eneuf. And when Hartley was laid by at t' last, Muster Wudsworth com doon ivery day to see him, and took communion wi' him at t' last.'

'Then Mr. Wordsworth and Hartley Coleridge were great friends?' I asked.

'Nay, nay, I doant think li'le Hartley ever set much by him, nevver was verra friendly, I doubt. Ye see, he [Mr. Wordsworth] was sae hard upon him, sae verra hard upon him, gev him sae much hard preaching aboot his ways.'

'Well, but Mrs. Wordsworth was kind to Hartley?' I said.

'Mappen she was bit I nivver saw it. She was' [and here the old man spoke very deliberately, as if this was the firmest conviction of his life]—'she was verra on-pleasant, vara on-pleasant indeed. A close-fisted woman, that's what she was.' But further inquiry elicited the reason of this personal dislike to the poet's wife, and a narrative of it will probably win a public verdict for the lady of Rydal Mount, with damages for libel against the man who so faithfully kep' li'le Hartley at the Nab, and so made his lodger's wrongs his own.

'Well, you see,' he continued gravely, 'I mind yance I went up to t' Mount to exe for sattlement of account, for Mrs. Wudsworth paid for Hartley's keep, time he lodged at t' Nab, and I had fifteen shillings i' t' beuk agin Coleridge for moneys I'd lent him different times. And she was verra awkard and on-pleasant, and wouldn't sattle, ye kna, for she thowt that Hartley had been drinkin' wi' it. But,' he added, 'howiver, I wrote to his mother, as lived in London, and she wreat to me and tell't me I was to lend a shilling or two as Hartley wanted it, and efter that she sattled wi' me for his lodgment hersel', but Mrs. Wudsworth was verra on-pleasant.'

I was glad to change a subject that so distressed him, and asked how the poet was generally dressed, and of his habits. 'Wudsworth wore a Jem Crow, never seed him in a boxer in my life,—a Jem Crow and an auld blue cloak was his rig, and *as for his habits, he had noan,* niver knew him with a pot i' his hand, or a pipe i' his mouth. But,' continued he, 'he was a girt skäter for a' that'—(I didn't see the connection of ideas —pipes and beer don't generally make for good skating),— 'noan better i' these parts—could cut his own name upo' t' ice, could Mr. Wudsworth.'

Before rising to go, I asked, 'Which roads were the favourites of the poet?'

'Well, well, he was ter'ble fond of going along under Loughrigg and ower by t' Redbank, but he was niver nowt of a mountaineer, allus kep' aboot t' roads.'

This was a bit of news I had not expected, but we will bear it in mind, and test its truth in future conversations with the poet's peasant contemporaries.

Our next talk shall be with one of the most well-informed of the Westmoreland builders, and I am indebted to Wordsworth's love of skating for an introduction to him. For making inquiries as to this pastime of the poet, I had chanced to hear how that Wordsworth had gone on one occasion to figure a bit by himself upon the White Moss Tarn. How that a predecessor of my friend the builder who lived near White Moss Tarn had sent a boy to sweep the snow from the ice for him, and how that when the boy returned from his labour he had asked him, 'Well, did Mr. Wudsworth gie ye owt?' and how that the boy with a grin of content from ear to ear had rejoined, 'Nay, bit I seed him tummle, tho'!'

I determined to seek out the builder and have the story first-hand, and was well repaid; for I heard something of the poet's gentle ways that was better than the grotesquely humorous answer of the boy who saw him fall.

The poet's skate had caught on a stone when he was in full swing, and he came with a crash on to the ice that starred the tarn and the lad, who had thought 'the tummle' a fair exchange for no pay, had been impressed with the quiet way in which Wordsworth had borne his fall. 'He didn't sweär nor say nowt, but he just sot up and said, 'Eh boy, that was a bad fall, wasn't it?' And now we are walking along briskly towards Grisedale, with the recounter of the story: 'Kna Wudsworth! I kent him weel,—why, he larnt me and William Brown to skäte. He was a ter'ble girt skater, was Wudsworth now; and he would put ya hand i' his breast (he wore a frill shirt i' them daays), and t'other hand i' his wäistband, same as shepherds dea to keep their hands warm, and he would stand up straight and swaay and swing away grandly.'

'Was he fond of any other pastime?' I asked.

'Naay, naay, he was ower feckless i' his hands. I nivver seed him at t' feasts, or wrestling, he hadn't owt of Christopher Wilson in him. Nivver was on wheels in his life, and wad rayther ha' been a tailor upon horseback happen, but he was a gey good un on t' ice, wonderful to see, could cut his neame upon it, I've hard tell, but nivver seed him do it.'

So that the rapture of the time when as a boy on Esthwaite's frozen lake Wordsworth had

> Wheeled about,
> Proud and exulting like an untired horse
> That cares not for his home, and shod with steel,
> Had hissed along the polished ice,

was continued into manhood's later day; and here was proof that the skill which the poet had gained, when

> Not seldom from the uproar he retired,
> Unto a silent bay, or sportively
> Glanced sideway, leaving the tumultous throng
> To cut across the reflex of a star,

was of such a kind as to astonish the natives among whom he dwelt.

My friend had known Wordsworth well, and what was better, knew his poems too. 'Here is t' verra spot, you'll mappen hev read it i' t' beuk, where Wudsworth saw Barbara feeding her pet lamb. She tell't me hersel. I was mending up t' cottage there at t' time. Eh, she was a bonny lass! they were a fine family a' t' lot o' Lewthwaites. She went lang sen and left, but she tell't me t' spot wi' her ain lips.' As I peered through the hedge upon the high-raised field at my right, I remembered that Barbara Lewthwaite's lips were for ever silent now, and recalled how I had heard from the pastor of a far-away parish that he had been asked by a very refined-looking handsome woman, on her death-bed, to read over to her and to her husband the poem of *The Pet Lamb*, and how she had said at the end, 'That was written about me. Mr. Wordsworth often spoke to me, and patted my head when I was a child,' and had added with a sigh, 'Eh, but he was such a dear kind old man.'

We passed on in silence till we were near 'Boon beck,' and opposite Greenhead ghyll, 'That,' said my companion, 'is a cottage as we used to ca' i' these parts t' Village Clock. Yan, I'se fergitten his neame, a shep, lived here, and i' winter days fowks fra far eneuf round wad say, "Is t' leet oot i' t' shep's cottage?" then you may wind t' clock and cover t' fire (for you kna matches was scarce and coal to fetch i' them days); and of a morning "Is t' leet i' t' winder? is t' shep stirrin'?" then ye maunt lig nea langer," we used to saay.' My friend did not know that this too was in 't' beuk,' as he called it,—that Wordsworth had described "the cottage on a spot of rising ground."

> And from its constant light so regular,
> And so far seen, the House itself, by all
> Who dwelt within the limits of the vale,
> Both old and young, was named the Evening Star.

Onward we trudged, entered the pastures leading to the Grasmere Common that stretches up to the Grisedale Pass, there sat, and had a talk as follows, the Tongue Ghyll Beck murmuring among the budding trees at our feet:

'Why, why, Wudsworth nevver said much to t' fowk, quite different fra lile Hartley, as knawed t' inside o' t' cottages for miles round, and was welcome i' them a'. He was distant, ye may saäy, verra distant. He wasn't made much count on "nayther i' these parts," but efter a time fwoaks began to

26

tak his advice, ye kna, aboot trees, and plantin', and cuttin', and buildin' chimleys, and that mak o' things. He hed his say at t' maist o' t' houses i' these parts, and was verra particler fond of round chimleys.'

It was delicious this description of the path to fame among his countrymen the poet had taken, but my friend explained himself as he went on:

'He was yan as keppit his heäd doon and eyes upo' t' ground, and mumbling to hissel; but why, why, he 'ud never pass folks draining, or ditching, or walling a cottage, but what he'd stop and say, "Eh dear, but it's a pity to move that stean, and doant ya think ya might leave that tree?"[1] I mind there was a walling chap just going to shoot a girt stean to bits wi' powder i' t' grounds at Rydal, and he came up and saaved it, and wreat summat on it.'

'But what was his reason,' I asked, 'for stopping the wallers or ditchers, or tree-cutters, at their work?'

'Well, well, he couldn't bide to see t' faäce o' things altered,[1] ye kna. It was all along of him that Grasmere folks have their Common open. Ye may ga now reet up t' sky ower Grizedale, wi'out liggin' leg to t' fence, and all through him. He said it was a pity to enclose it and run walls over it, and the quality backed him, and he won. Fwoaks was angry eneuf, and wreat rhymes aboot it; but why, why, it's a deal pleasanter for them as walks up Grisedale, ye kna, let alean reets o' foddering and goosage for freemen i' Gersmer.'

'But Mr. Wordsworth was a great critic at trees. I've seen him many a time lig o' his back for long eneuf to see whedder a branch or a tree sud gang or not. I mind weel I was building Kelbarrer for Miss S——, and she telt me I med get to kna Wudsworth's 'pinion. Sea I went oop til him as he com i' t' way, and he said, "Ay, ay, t' building wad dea, and t' site wad, but it's verra bare, verra bare."

'I mind anudder time I was building t' hoose aboon Town

[1]Readers who may chance to have seen the letter Wordsworth wrote to the local paper when he heard the news of the first railway invasion of the Lake district, will notice how accurately true this piece of testimony is.

End, wi' a lock of trees and planting round, and he said to me, "Well, well, you're fifty years in advance here": he meant it was grawed up weel.

'And I mind yance upon a time at Hunting Stile thereaway he coomed up. "Now, Mr. Wudsworth, how will it goa?" I said. He answered me, "It'll dea; but where are the trees?" and I said, "Oh, it's weel eneuf for trees, it nobbut wants its whiskers." "How so?" said he. "Why, it's a young 'un," I said, "and we doant blame a young 'un for not hevin' it's hair upo' it's faace." And he laughed, and he said, "Very good, a very good saying; very true, very true." But he was ter'ble jealous of new buildings.

'As for Mrs. Wudsworth, why, why, she was a verra plain woman, plainest i' these parts, and she was a manasher an' aw, and kepp t' accounts. For ye kna he nivver knew aboot sec things, nayder what he had or what he spent.'

As we rose to continue our climb, my friend looked at the trees in the little stream-bed below us, and said, 'In my days there was a deal of wild fruit in these parts. We hed toffee feasts i' t' winter, and cherry feasts i' t' summer,—gey big gedderings at t' cherry feasts.'

'Did you ever see Wordsworth at one?'

'Nivver, he nobbut followed ya amusement: that was skating, as I telt ye.'

'Had he any particular friends among the shepherds?' I asked.

'Nay, nay, not as ever I kent or heard on; but he wozn't a mountaineer, was maistly doon below aboot t' road.'

'But what was his favourite road?'

'Oh, roond by Gersmere and t' Red Bank and heam again, wiowt ony doubt. He wad gang twice i' t' day roond by Mr. Barber's there. He was a girt walker roond there, and a'most as girt a eater. Why, why, he wad git breakfast at heam, poddish or what not, and then come wi' Miss Wudsworth roond t' lake to Mr. Barber's, and fall in wi' them, and then off and roond agean, and be at Barber's at tea-time and supper up agean before gaen heam. And as for her, why, Miss Wudsworth, she wad often come into t' back kitchen and exe for a bit of oatcake and butter. She was fond of oatcake, and butter till it, fit to stëal it a'most. Why, why, but she was a ter'ble cliver woman, was that. She did as much of his potry as he did, and went completely off it at the latter end wi' studying it, I suppose. It's a verra straange thing, noo, that studying didn't run on i' t' family.'

It was, I thought, a little hard to expect that the poet should have handed on the torch, or to speak with disrespect of his sons because they only thought in prose. But it was evidence that my friend, at least, of a profound belief in the genius of the Rydal poet and tree-and-building critic of old days. And it would have been a guess shrewdly made that it was Wordsworth's brotherhood with him, in the interests of his builder life, and jealous care for architecture in the vales, that had made the bond so strong and the belief in the poet so great, and exclusive. We descended into the valley, took tea together at the Swan Inn, and chatted on: now learning that Wordsworth was a regular attendant at Grasmere Church, now that he would often in church-time be like a dazed man,—forget to stand up and sit down, turn right round and stare vacantly at the congregation. 'But I mind ya daay perticler, when he and Hartley and I cam oot o' t' church tagedder. I said, "What did you think of the sermon, Mr. Wudsworth?" and he answered me, "Oh, it was verra good and verra plain"; and I said, "Saame here, Mr. Wudsworth"; and li'le Hartley put his heëad o' ya side, and squeaked out, "Oh, did ye think it was good? well, well, I was in purgatory the whole time." '

The stars were overhead as we left all that was left—and that was little enough—of our cosy evening meal; and, bidding good-night, I went home, with more Wordsworth memories to keep me company.

It was by happy accident that I was enabled to have a chat with one of the best types of our half-farmer, half hotel-keeper, only a few days before he left the Rydal neighbourhood for good, after a sojourn of sixty-five years therein. We met at the house of a friend where he had been to pay his last rent due, and as I entered the room I was conscious of a be-whiskied conversationally aromatic air that boded well for a reet doon good crack.

'Kna Wudsworth! I sud kna him, if any man sud, for as a lad I carried t' butter to t' Mount, as a grawin' man I lived and worked in seet on him, and I lig noo upon t' verra bed-stocks as he and his missus ligged on when they were first wed, and went to Town End theereaway.'

'Now tell me,' said I, 'what was the poet like in face and make?'

'Well in mak he was listyish. I dar say I cud gee him four inches, now I suddent wonder but what I could, mysen.' My informant stood about six feet four, or four and a half. 'He was much to leuk at like his son William; he was a listy man was his son, mind ye. But for a' he was a sizeable man, was t' fadder, he was plainish featured, and was a man as hed nea pleasure in his faace. Quite different Wudsworth was fra li'le Hartley. Hartley allus hed a bit of smile or a twinkle in his faace, but Wudsworth was not loveable i' t' faace by nea means, for o' he was sizeable man, mind ye.'

'But,' I interrupted, 'was he not much like your friend John Rigg in face?'

'He med be t' seame mak, ye kna, much aboot; but, John Rigg hes a bit pleasant in his faace at wust o' times, and Wudsworth bless ye, never had noan.'

'Was he,' I said, 'a sociable man, Mr. Wordsworth, in the earliest times you can remember?'

'Wudsworth,' my kindly giant replied, 'for a' he hed nea pride nor nowt, was a man who was quite one to hissel, ye kna. He was not a man as fwoaks could crack wi', nor not a man as could crack wi' fwoaks. But thear was anudder thing as kep' fwoaks off, he hed a terr'ble girt deep voice, and ye med see his faace agaan for lang eneuf. I've knoan folks, village lads and lasses, coming ower by t' auld road aboon what runs fra Gersmer to Rydal, flayt a'most to death there by t' Wishing Gate to hear t' girt voice a groanin' and mutterin' and thunderin' of a still evening. And he hed a way of standin' quite still by t' rock there in t' path under Rydal, and fwoaks could hear sounds like a wild beast coming frat' rocks, and childer were scared fit to be dëad a'most.'

'He was a great walker, I know,' I broke in. 'Which were his favourite roads? and was he generally on the hills, or did he keep pretty much to the valleys?'

'He was a gey good walker, an' for a' he hed latterly a pony and phaeton, I nevver yance seed him in a conveyance in t' whole o' my time. But he was niver a mountain man. He wad gae a deal by Pelter-bridge and round by Red Bank, but he was maist terr'ble fond o' under t' Nab, and by t' auld high road to t' Swan Inn and back, and verra often came as far as Dungeon Ghyll. You've happen heered tell o' Dungeon Ghyll; it was a verra favourite spot o' Wudsworth's, noo, was that, and he yance med some potry aboot a lamb as fell ower. And I dar say it was true eneuf a' but t' rhymes, and ye kna they war put in to help it oot.'

For the life of me, as he spoke, I didn't understand whether he meant that the rhymes fished the lamb out of the Dungeon Ghyll pool, or helped the poet out with his verses, but I suppressed a smile and listened attentively.

'But for a' he was a distant man, they war weel spoken on, mind ye, at the Mount,' continued my voluble friend. 'They stood high, and he was a man as paid his way and settled verra reglar; not that his potry brought him in much, a deal wasn't made up in beuks till efter he was dëad. Ay, and they lived weel. Many's the time, when I was a lad, and I went wid butter, I could ha' been weel content to be let aloan for a bit i' t' pantry. 'Ticing things there, mind ye. And they kep' three sarvants. I kent t' cook and t' housemaid weel, and yan they called Dixon, smart lile chap as iver was seen in these parts, but ter'ble given over to cauld watter and temperance —he woz. Coomed out of a "union," but verra neat, and always a word for onybody, and a verra quiet man, particlar quiet, nivver up to nea mischief, and always sat at heam wi' t' lasses a mending and sewing o' evenings, ye kna.'

I didn't know, but guessed at once the sort of simple stayat-home ways and happy-family style of quiet domestic service, known to the circle of maidens, who, after their day's work, sat with their needles and thread entertaining the guileless Dixon.

'And what is your memory of Mrs. Wordsworth?'

'Well, every Jack mun have his Jen, as t' saying is, and they was much of a mak. She was a stiff little lady, nowt verra pleasant in her countenance neyther.' I soon found out that the word unpleasant was being used in a double sense, and was intended to convey rather an over-seriousness of expression perhaps than any disagreeable look or ill-tempered face. 'Ye're weel awar',' continued the former hostel-keeper, 'that we mun a' hev troubles, times is not a' alike wi' t' best on us; we hev our worrits and our pets, but efter yan on 'em, yan's countenance comes agean, and Wudsworth's didn't, nor noan o' t' family's, as I ivver seed.'

'Did you ever see Mr. Wordsworth out walking—round Pelter-bridge way?'

'Ay, ay, scores and scores o' times. But he was a lonely man, fond o' goin' out wi' his family, and saying nowt to noan of 'em. When a man goes in a family way he keeps together wi' 'em and chats a bit wi' 'em, but many's a time I've seed him a takkin' his family out in a string, and niver geein' the deariest bit of notice to 'em; standin' by hissel' and stoppin' behint agapin', wi' his jaws warkin' the whoal time; but niver no cracking wi' 'em, nor no pleasure in 'em,—a desolate-minded man, ye kna. Queer thing that, mun, but it was his hobby, ye kna. It was potry as did it. We all hev our hobbies—somes for huntin', some cardin', some fishin', some wrustlin'. He never followed nowt nobbut a bit o' skating, happen. Eh, he was fond of going on in danger times;—he was always furst on t' Rydal howiver; but his hobby, ye mun kna, was potry. It was a queer thing, but it would like eneuf cause him to be desolate; and I'se often thowt that his brain was that fu' of sic stuff, that he was forced to be always at it whether or no, wet or fair, mumbling to hissel' along t' roads.'

'Do you think,' I asked, 'that he had any friends among the shepherds?'

'Naay, naay, he cared nowt about fwoak, nor sheep, nor dogs (he hed a girt fine yan, weighed nine stone, to guard t' hoose) not nea mair than he did aboot t' claes he hed on—his hobby was potry.'

'How did he generally dress?'

'Well, in my time them swallow-lappeted yans was in vogue, but he kep' to all-round plain stuff, and I mind hed a cap wi' a neb tull it. He wore that maist days.'

'Did you ever read his poetry, or see any books about it in the farm-houses?' I asked.

'Ay, ay, time or two. But ya're weel aware there's potry and potry. There's potry wi' a li'le bit pleasant in it, and potry sec as a man can laugh at or t' childer understand, and some as taks a deal o' mastery to mak' oot what's said, and a deal of Wudsworth's was this sort, ye kna. You cud tell fra t' man's faace his potry wad nivver hev nea laugh in it.

'His potry was quite different wark frae li'le Hartley. Hartley wad gang runnin' beside o' t' becks and mak his, and gang in t' furst open deur and write what he hed gittin' on t' paper. But Wudsworth's potry was real hard stuff, and bided a deal of makkin', and he'd keep it in his heäd for lang eneuf. Eh, but it's queer, mon, different ways fwoaks hes of makkin' potry now. Fowks gaes a deal to see whar he's interred; but for my part I'd walk twice distance ower t' Fells to see whar Hartley lies. Not bit what Mr. Wudsworth didn't stand verra high, and was a weel-spoken man eneuf, but quite yan to hissel. Well, well, good-day.' And so we rose to go; he to his farm, I to my notebook.

I pass over sundry interviews of minor import, and will detail as accurately as I can the result of several conversations with one who as a boy lived as page, or butler's assistant, at Rydal Mount, and now himself in total eclipse (for he is blind) delights to handle and show with pride the massy, old-fashioned square glazed hand-lantern, that lighted his master the poet on his favourite evening walks.

We go through Ambleside to reach his house, and call for a moment at the shop of a man for whom on his wedding-day Hartley Coleridge wrote the touching sonnet in which he describes himself as

Untimely old, irreverendly grey,

and he will tell us that Mr. Wordsworth was not a man of very outgoing ways with folk, a plain man, a very austere man, and one who was ponderous in his speech. That he called very often at his shop, and would talk, 'but not about much,' just passing the day. He will tell us that Mrs Wordsworth was a very plain-faced lady, but will add that, 'for aw that, Mr. Wordsworth and she were very fond of one another.'

There is, as one would expect, a sort of general feeling among the dalesmen that it was rather a strange thing that two people so austere and uncomely in mere line of feature or figure should be so much in love, and so gentle and considerate in their lives. I say as we should expect, for the men of Lakeland and the women of Lakeland are notably comely, their features notably regular. I do not myself know of a single instance of a really ugly married woman among the peasants that I have met with in Westmoreland. But at the same time we must remember that the word 'plain,' whether applied to dress or feature, in Westmoreland, means for the most part simple, homely, unpretending, unassuming, and is often a term of honour rather than dispraise.

We shall, perhaps, as we near the village where our blind friend lives, meet with an old man who will tell us that he helped to bear both the poet and his wife to the grave, but he will add that he was not 'over weel acquent wi' 'em, though he knas the room they both died in,' and that the time he saw most of the poet was the occasion when he conducted Queen Adelaide 'to see the Rydal Falls, and all about.'

We have got to the end of our walk, and here, picking his

way by means of his trusty sounding-staff backwards and forwards in the sunshine he feels, but cannot see, is the old man, or rather old gentleman who in former times 'took sarvice along of Mr. Wudsworth,' and was 'so well pleased with his master that he could verra weel hev ended his days at t' Mount,' but found it was over quiet, and, wanting to see the world beyond the charmed circle of the hills, left a good place, but not before he had formed his opinion of both master and mistress, and obtained indelible impressions of their several personalities, and had conceived along with these an affection for them which glows in his words as he talks to us of them. 'Mr. Wudsworth was a plaain-feaced man, and a mean liver.' The description, as I hinted in the preface, would have staggered a philo-Wordsworthian unaccustomed to the native dialect. 'But he was a good master and kind man; and as for Mrs. Wudsworth, she was a downright cliver woman, as kep' accounts, and was a reg'lar manasher. He never know'd, bless ye, what he hed, nor what he was wuth, nor whether there was owt to eat in t' house, nivver.'

'But you say,' I interposed, 'that he didn't care much whether there was or was not food in the house.'

'Nay, nay, Wudsworth was a man as was fond of a good dinner at times, if you could get him to it, that was t' job; not but what he was a very temperate man i' all things, vara, but they was all on 'em mean livers, and in a plain way. It was poddish for t' breakfast, and a bit o' mutton to t' dinner, and poddish at night, with a bit of cheese happen to end up wi'.'

'You said it was hard to get him to his meals: what did you mean?' I asked.

'Weel, weel, it was study as was his delight: he was aw for study; and Mrs. Wudsworth would say, "Ring the bell," but he wouldn't stir, bless ye. "Goa and see what he's doing," she'd say, and we wad goa up to study door and hear him a mumbling and bumming through it. "Dinner's ready, sir," I'd ca' out, but he'd goa mumbling on like a deaf man, ya see. And sometimes Mrs. Wudsworth 'ud say, "Goa and brek a bottle, or let a dish fall just outside door in passage." Eh dear,

35

that maistly wad bring him out, wad that. It was nobbut that as wad, howivver. For ye kna he was a verra careful man, and he couldn't do with brekking t' china.'

'And was he continually at study in-doors, or did he rise early, go out for a walk before breakfast, and study, as I have heard, mostly in the open air?' I asked.

My friend answered at once. 'He was always at it, ye kna, but it was nowt but what he liked, and not much desk-wark except when he had a mind tul it. Noa, noa, he was quite a open-air man was Wudsworth: studied a deal aboot t' roads. He wasn't particlar fond of gitten up early, but did a deal of study efter breakfast, and a deal efter tea. Walked t' roads efter dark, he wad, a deal, between his tea and supper, and efter. Not a verra conversable man, a mumblin' and stoppin', and seein' nowt nor neabody.'

'And what were his favourite roads?' I asked, in an innocent way.

'Well, he was verra partial to ganging up to Tarn Foot in Easedale, and was fondest o' walking by Red Bank and round by Barber's (the late Miss Agar's house), or else t'other way about and home by Clappersgate and Brankers, under Lough-rigg. Never was nowt of a mountaineer, and Miss Dorothy 'companied him. Eh dear, many time I've watched him coming round wi' t' lantern and her efter a walk by night. You've heard tell of Miss Dorothy, happen. Well, fwoaks said she was cliverest mon of the two at his job, and he allays went to her when he was puzzelt. Dorothy hed t' wits, tho' she went wrang, ye kna.'

'Then,' said I, 'Mrs. Wordsworth did not help the poet in writing his verses?'

'Naay, naay. Why, she was a manasher, niver a studier, but for a' that there's nea doot he and she was truly companionable, and they wer terr'ble fond o' yan anudder. But Dorothy hed t' wits on 'em boath.'

'And he was very devoted to his children,' I put in.

'Ay, ay, he was fond of children like eneuf, but children was nivver verra fond o' him. Ye see he was a man 'o moods, nivver nea certainty aboot him; and I'se not sea sure he was fond of other fwok's bairns, but he was verra fond o' his ain wi'out a doot.'

'And was he very popular among the folk hereabouts?'

'There's nea doot but what he was fond of quality, and quality was very fond o' him, but he niver exed fowk aboot their wark, not noticed t' flocks nor nowt: not but what he was a kind man if fwoaks was sick and taen badly. But farming, nor beast, nor sheep, nor fields wasn't in his way, he exed nea questions about flocks or herds, and was a distant man, not what you might call an outward man by noa means. And he was verra close, verra close indeed, fra curious men. He'd gang t' other side o' t' road rather than pass a man as exed questions a deal.'

It was a mercy, I thought to myself, that no Wordsworth Society had invited me to collect and write down the results of a cross-question tour in those days.

'But surely,' I said, 'he had some particular cottage or farm where he would go and have a crack.'

'Naay, naay. He would go times or two to farm Dungeon Ghyll way, but he wasn't a man for friends. He had some, neäh doubt, in his walk of life; he was ter'ble friends with the Doctor (Arnold) and Muster Southey, and Wilson of Elleray and Hartley Coleridge. I'se seen him many a time takkin' him out arm i' arm for a talking. But he was specially friendly with Professor. I mind one time when we was driving, me and Mrs. Wudsworth and Miss Wudsworth, to Kendal, and Professor Wilson was superintending making o' a bye road up by Elleray there, and he was in his slippers. Nowt wud do but Wudsworth must git down and fall to talkin', and we went on; but he didn't come, and Mrs. Wudsworth said, 'Ye mun drive on; he'll pick us up at Kendal: no knowing what's got him now Professor is wi' 'im.' Well, well, she was right. For after putting up at Kendal, who should walk in but Wudsworth and Professor wi'out any shoes to his feet neäther, for Wilson was in his slippers, and 'ad walk'd hissel' to his stockin' feet, and left his stockin' on t' road an aw' far eneuf before they got to Kendal.'

'But it was strange,' I said again in a suggestive way, 'that Mr. Wordsworth should be so well "acquaint" with Professor Wilson, for he was a great cock-fighting and wrestling man, was he not, in his day?'

'Ay, ay, biggest hereaboot,' my old friend replied. 'It's queer, but it was along o' his study, ye kna. Wudsworth was nivver nea cock-fyhter nor wrestler, no gaming man at all, and not a hunter, and as for fishing he hedn't a bit o' fish in him, hedn't Wudsworth—not a bit of fish in him.'

'I have read in his books,' said I, 'things that make me feel he was kind to dumb animals.'

'Naay, naay,' my friend broke in, 'Wudsworth was nea dog fancier; and as for cats, he couldn't abide them; and he didn't care for sheep, or horses, a deal, but if he was fond of owt, it was of t' *li'le ponies*. He was a man of fancies, ye kna. It was a fancy of his. He was fond of li'le ponies, nivver rode a horse in his life, nivver.'

'But he went over a deal of ground in his time. Was he always on his feet?' I said.

'He went ower a deal mair ground nor ever he saw, for he went a deal by night, but he was a man as took notice, ye kna, nivver forgat what he saw, and he went slow.'

'But,' said I, 'how did he cover so much ground; was he never on wheels?'

'Ay, ay, wheels, to be sure, he druv a' times, ya kna, in t' cart. He, and Mrs. Wudsworth, and Dorothy and me, we went a deal by cart Penrith way, and Borradale and Keswick way, and Langdale way at times.'

'What sort of a cart?' I inquired.

'Dung cart, to be sure. Just a dung cart, wi' a seat-board in t' front, and bit of bracken in t' bottom, comfortable as owt. We cud ga that way for days, and far eneuf. Ye kna in them days tubs wasn't known. Low-wood was nobbut a cottage, and there was never abuv six or seven ponies for hiring at Ambleside. Tubs we ca' t' covered carriages, tubs wasn't known in these parts. But happen there was a tub or two at Kendal.'

'And you must have gone precious slowly,' I said.

'Ay, ay, slow eneuf, but that was Mr. Wudsworth's fancy, and he'd git in and go along, and then he git down into t' road and walk a bit, and mak a bit, and then he git oop and hum a bit to himsel, and then he'd stop and hev a leuk here and there for a while. He was a man as noticed a deal o' steans and trees, verra particler aboot t' trees, or a rock wi' ony character in it. When they cut down coppy woods in these parts they maistly left a bit of t' coppy just behint wall to hide it for him, he was a girt judge in sic things, and noticed a dëal.'

'And would he,' I asked, 'tell you as you jogged along in the cart, which mountain he was fondest off, or bid you look at the sunset?'

'Ay, ay, times he would say, "Now isn't that beautiful?" and times he would hum on to himself. But he wasn't a man as would give judgment agean ony mountain. I've heard girt folks 'at com to t' Mount say, "Now, Mr. Wudsworth, we want to see finest mountain in t' country," and he would say, "Ivery mountain is finest." Ay, that's what he would say.'

'But I have been told that his voice was very deep,' I put in, in a happy-go-lucky way. 'Had he a loud laugh now?'

'I don't mind he iver laughed in his life, he'd smile times or two. Ay, ay, his voice was deep one; bit I mind at t' family prayers in t' morning he'd read a bit o' *the* Scripture to us, and he was a verra articulate, particlar good reader, was Mr. Wudsworth, always hed family prayer in the morning, and went to church wi' prayer-book under his arm, verra regular yance upon the Sunday, he did.' My friend added, 'He was quite a serious-minded man, and a man of moods.'

Here ended my talk with the old retainer at the Mount. But I was not allowed to go off until I had seen and handled the old-fashioned candle lattern by which, as my kind informant put it, the poet 'did a deal of his study aboot t' roads efter dark.'

And so must end my plain unvarnished tale. I leave my

indulgent readers to form their own conclusions; merely suggesting that the collected evidence points to a simple plainness and homeliness of life such as remains indelibly impressed upon the men of Westmoreland, whose own lives are less simple in these latter days, when ostentation and vulgar pride of wealth in a class above them have climbed the hills and possessed the valleys.

The testimony of the witnesses I have been fortunate enough to bring before you seems to agree in depicting Wordsworth as he painted himself, a plain man, continually murmuring his undersong as he passed along by brook and woodland, pacing the ground with unuplifted eye, but so retired, that even the North country peasant, who does even yet recognise the social differences of class and caste that separate and divide 'the unknown little from the unknowing great,' was unable to feel at home with him. 'Not a very companionable man at the best of times' was their verdict. But I think all the while these dalesmen seem to have felt that if the poet was not of much count as a worldly-wise farm or shepherd authority, nor very convivial and free and easy as li'le Hartley was, nor very athletic and hearty as Professor Wilson, there was a something in the severe-faced, simply habited man 'as said nowt to neabody' that made him head and shoulders above the people, and bade them listen and remember when he spoke, if it was only on the lopping of a tree or the building of a chimney-stack. 'He was a man of a very practical eye, and seemed to see everything,' was the feeling.

And turning from the poet to his wife, whilst one can see how the household need of economy in early Town End days gave her to the last the practical power of household management that had almost passed into a proverb, one can see also how true was that picture of the

Being breathing thoughtful breath,
. . . . .
A perfect woman, nobly planned,
To warn, to comfort, and command.

'He never knawed, they say, what he was wuth, nor what he hed i' t' house.' She did it all. Then, too, it is touching to notice how deep and true the constant love between man and wife was seen to be, how truly companions for life they were, and that, too, in the eyes of a class of people who never saw that

> Beauty born of murmuring sound
> Had passed into her face,

and half marvelled that the spirit wed with spirit was so marvellously closer than fleshly bond to flesh.

Upright, the soul of honour, and for that reason standing high with all; just to their servants; well meaning and quiet in their public life; full of affection in their simple home life; so it seems the poet and his wife lived and died. Thought a deal of for the fact that accounts were strictly met at the tradesmen's shops, they were thought more of because they were ever ready to hear the cry of the suffering, and to enter the doors of those ready to perish.

I do not think I have been able to tell the world anything new about the poet or his surroundings. But the man 'who hedn't a bit of fish in him, and was no mountaineer,' seems to have been in the eyes of the people always at his studies; 'and that because he couldn't help it, because it was his hobby,' for sheer love, and not for money. This astonished the industrious money-loving folk, who could not understand the doing work for 'nowt,' and perhaps held the poet's occupation in somewhat lighter esteem, just because it did not bring in 'a deal o' brass to the pocket.' I think it is very interesting, however, to notice how the woman part of the Rydal Mount family seemed to the simple neighbourhood to have the talent and mental ability; and there must have been, both about Dorothy Wordsworth and the poet's daughter Dora, a quite remarkable power of inspiring the minds of the poor with whom they came in contact, with a belief in their intellectual faculties and brightness and cleverness. If Hartley Coleridge was held by some to be Wordsworth's helper, it was to Dorothy he was supposed by all to turn if 'ivver he was puzzelt.' The

women had 'the wits, or best part of 'em.'—this was prover-
bial among the peasantry, and, as having been an article of
rural faith, it has been established out of the mouths of all
the witnesses it has been my lot to call.

Printed in an edition of 2000 copies

The Anchor Press Limited
Tiptree, Colchester, Essex.

Text set in 12 pt Monotype Fournier

Binding by William Brendon Ltd.

Paper: Abbey Mills Suede 107 G.S.M.

Endpapers: Tumba Ingre

Designed by Eric Ayers